KidLit-O Presents

Career As A Firefighter

What They Do, How to Become One, and
What the Future Holds!

Brian Rogers

KidLit-O Books

www.kidlito.com

© 2013. All Rights Reserved.

Cover Image © Duncan Noakes - Fotolia.com

Table of Contents

About KidCaps

KidLit-O is an imprint of BookCaps™ that is just for kids! Each month BookCaps will be releasing several books in this exciting imprint. Visit are website or like us on Facebook to see more!

A firefighter putting out a large fire at a house[1]

Introduction

What does it mean to be a hero? For most people, a hero is someone who helps others at considerable expense to himself or to herself. Some people might imagine that a hero is someone who is there right when they are needed most- someone who solves the tough problems and who doesn't ask for anything in return. Although the movies might make us think that a person needs to have special powers to be a hero, in this book we will talk about the kind of everyday hero that you have seen with your own two eyes: a firefighter.

Have you ever felt a rush of excitement when you see a bright red fire truck go speeding down the road with its lights flashing and its loud horn honking? All the cars on the road have to pull over to let the fire truck pass by, and if the truck is on its way to an emergency, then it won't even stop for red lights! Have you ever wondered what it would be like to be on that truck with those firefighters, speeding to the rescue for someone in your community?

Firefighters are true heroes that you can see every day. They work long hours each and every week, and they do not ask for special attention. They are usually among the first to arrive on the scene of an accident, and they are highly trained to be able to help in many different types of emergencies. Often, when everyone else is trying to run out of a burning building, the firefighters are the ones running into it to save the people trapped inside.

But what kind of training did the men and women who became firefighters have to receive? What is a typical day like for a firefighter and what can you do to get ready for a career as a firefighter? In this book, we will be looking at what it is like to work as a firefighter by reading in detail about seven different areas. After you have finished this book, you will have a better idea of whether or not being a firefighter is the right career for you.

The first area that we will talk about is what exactly is involved in being a firefighter. What is expected of each firefighter and what kind of reputation should each one have? As with many jobs, there is often a significant difference between what people think firefighters do and what the reality of the matter is. You will see how firefighters around the world play an important role in the communities that they serve.

Then we will learn about the specialized training that each person has to go through before they can become a firefighter. The training involves both the mind and the body, and each potential firefighter is expected to have a high level of physical performance and a working knowledge of their field. How long does the training last and how many people successfully complete it? We will find out in the second section.

The third section will show us some of the reality of being a firefighter by answering the question: is it an easy job? We will talk about some of the unique conditions that firefighters have to deal with. See if you can figure out whether or not just anyone can walk in off the street and start working as a firefighter. From the long hours to the sad things that they see sometimes, there are some specific challenges that firefighters have to live with.

Then the fourth section will give us an exciting look at the average day of a firefighter. We will get to stay at the stationhouse with a crew, ride along with them as they answer emergency calls, and participate in the many different parts of being a firefighter. While you probably have an idea of what a firefighter does with their time all day, you may be surprised to find out that being a firefighter is more than just running into burning buildings. For example, did you know that a firefighter has to mow lawns and clean toilets during their shift?

The fifth section will talk honestly about the hardest part of being a firefighter. Although firefighters are expected to keep the stationhouse clean, to work long hours, and to be in superb physical shape, the hardest part for most firefighters is something altogether unrelated to the actual work- some firefighters have trouble dealing with the tragedies of life that they come across in their jobs. Firefighters have to see some terrible things sometimes, and it's not always easy to control the emotions that come up. This section will talk openly about the darker side of being a firefighter.

Then, in the sixth section, we will look down the road into the future to try and see what the career of a firefighter will be like in ten years, right about the time that you might consider signing up yourself. What kinds of new technologies will be available and how will the job change? Will firefighters still be needed in ten years? You will probably be fascinated with the answers to those questions.

Lastly, the seventh and final section will answer the important question: "How can I get ready now to become a firefighter". Even though a person must be at least eighteen years old in most states to become a firefighter, there are several things that you can do right now to get ready. We will talk about how you can prepare yourself physically and mentally right now, so that when you are eighteen you can start the process to become a firefighter.

The world today still needs heroes. There are lots of emergencies where innocent people get hurt and need someone to help them. Firefighters in every town are special because they are willing to give their time and energy to help their neighbors, no matter who these neighbors might be. Firefighters are a special type of person, and not everyone can do their job. So whether or not you decide to become a firefighter yourself after reading this book, try to use what you learn to appreciate what a difficult job these men and women have and how important they are to every town and city. We should all be thankful for the work that they do.

Let's start with the first section.

Chapter 1: What Is a firefighter?

As you can probably guess from the name, firefighters are often seen with axes and fire extinguishers trying to put out fires. Whether the fire is in the back of a restaurant, on the top floor of a skyscraper, or even on a boat in the middle of the ocean, trained firefighters are always ready to extinguish an out of control fire. In fact, when most people think of a firefighter, they think of a person dressed in heavy clothes wearing a mask and carrying a hose towards a burning building.

But in real life, firefighters do so much more.

Most firefighters are also trained paramedics. Do you know what a paramedic is? A paramedic is someone who helps out in medical emergencies until the victim can be cared for by doctors at a hospital. Paramedics usually work with ambulance services, helping victims of accidents and illnesses to arrive safely at a hospital. Paramedics have to think quickly to decide what is happening with the victim, how to start treating them, and how to safely transport them to a hospital. Many firefighters spend at least some time working as paramedics in ambulances until they can get a job as a firefighter.

Firefighters usually end up spending much of their time assisting victims of accidents and less time putting out fires. Firefighters are often the first ones to arrive on the scene of a car accident, so it is often their job to rescue people who are trapped inside their cars and to provide important first aid to anyone who has been hurt.

Firefighters also fill a variety of roles that help to keep the community safe. Some experienced firefighters become fire building inspectors. They travel around to different buildings in the area and make sure that they are safe. If there is too much clutter, problems with electrical or water systems, or too few fire extinguishers, they will make sure that the potentially dangerous problems get fixed. They will also make sure that each company has a detailed emergency evacuation plan in case of fire and that exit signs are easy to see for the employees who have to leave the building during an emergency.

Other experienced firefighters choose to become fire investigators. After a large fire, like one where a lot of property was destroyed or where someone died, one or more specially trained firefighters will be assigned to investigate what caused the fire by tracing the fire back to where it started. This is not an easy thing to do, but with special methods and mathematical formulas the investigators can find out where the fire started burning and whether or not any extra fuel (like gasoline) was used to make it burn hotter and faster. That will allow them to decide if the fire was an accident or if it was set on purpose by someone. In case the fire was set on purpose (a crime called "arson") then the firefighters will work together with the police to find and arrest the guilty person.

Firefighters can also receive special training to be the driver of a fire truck, an operator of different types of heavy equipment used in emergencies, to work with hazardous materials cleanup, or to use SCUBA gear during underwater rescues. When a firefighter has shown that they can keep control when under pressure and that they have a good understanding of how to handle emergencies, they can apply for a special job called "dispatcher", who is the person that uses a radio to direct different fire crews to the various emergencies in the area. The dispatcher has to know where each crew is located, which crews are available, what each crew is trained to do.

But firefighters don't just try to arrive on the scene after an accident or fire has happened- they also try to help their neighbors to avoid accidents and fires in the first place. Firefighters make a habit of visiting schools, businesses, and community centers to educate everyone there about fire safety and first aid. For example, a firefighter might visit your school and explain how to prevent a fire from starting. They might talk about the importance of not playing with matches and also what to in case of a fire. What will they say? They will demonstrate how to use a fire extinguisher and what to do in case the fire gets onto your clothes- STOP, DROP, and ROLL. They will also talk about the importance of crawling to safety away from a fire. These safety tips can help to save your life if you are ever in a fire.

While most people think about how brave firefighters are as they rush into a burning building, we have seen that firefighters do much more for their communities even when there are no emergencies. They inspect buildings to make sure that the conditions are safe, they investigate fires to see if there was any criminal activity, they dispatch emergency crews to help victims of accidents, and they instruct communities how to prevent fires and how to react in case a fire breaks out.

Even before an accident happens, firefighters are working hard to keep us safe.

Chapter 2: What Is the Training Like to Become a Firefighter?

To become a firefighter, a person must be at least eighteen years old and have graduated from high school (or have passed the General Educational Development [GED] tests). After that, they can start the process of beginning this exciting new career. Most interested people start by trying to educate themselves as much as they can to get ready for the written exam. Then, they focus on the physical exam (PAT-Physical Ability Test) and the oral interview.

Specialized education equips firefighters to deal with the many and different emergency situations that they might come across in a day's work. They must be ready to perform CPR, to cut someone out of a vehicle, to climb a ladder into a burning building, and to educate the public about fire safety. Firefighters aren't born with this important knowledge- they have to learn it just like everyone else. One helpful step that many future firefighters start with is receiving a specialized education at a local community college. They can usually take courses on fire technology (which discusses building structures and the behavior of fire) and human anatomy and physiology (which will help when giving first aid to victims). This valuable education gives future firefighters crucial knowledge for helping their communities.

In most areas, the next step is to attend a Fire Academy, where classes last for about eight hours a day for six months. Such intensive studying can be difficult for some people, and not everyone who starts the course will graduate. But those who endure the training will receive excellent practice learning all of the skills that they will need to save lives.

After finishing the six month Fire Academy, most firefighters will be required to learn how to become an Emergency Medical Technician (EMT) and perhaps even a Paramedic. This training can easily take another eight or nine months, meaning a total of about 15 months of instruction before being able to apply for a job as a firefighter.

Along with a good education, firefighters must also prepare themselves physically for the job. To make sure that interested people are up to the task, all candidates must pass an incredibly demanding physical test (the PAT) before being hired as a firefighter.

A candidate participating in the PAT[2]

What is the test like? In most areas, the physical test involves seeing if the candidate can perform well in eight areas[3]:

[2] Image source: http://www.youtube.com/watch?v=k3DLQDVBq50

[3] Physical test info source: http://lincoln.ne.gov/city/fire/employ/pat.pdf

- **Charged line advance** (pulling a heavy fire hose at least 90 feet)
- **Forcible entry simulation** (swinging a sledge hammer to move a target- to practice breaking open doors)
- **Equipment carry simulation** (a heavy piece of equipment must be carried for 100 feet without dropping it)
- **Ceiling breach and pull** (using a special tool, candidates must practice pushing and pulling heavy sections of a ceiling to check for fire)
- **Ladder heel** (a 24 foot ladder must be raised and lowered against a building)
- **Ladder raise** (another 24 foot ladder must be extended against the side of a building)
- **Stair climb with equipment** (the candidate must climb up a set of stairs carrying breathing equipment and a heavy hose)
- **Victim Rescue-dummy drag** (a 170 pound dummy must be dragged for 50 feet)

You can imagine how physically demanding this test is. However, to make sure that only the most physically fit candidates pass, a time limit is established- a little over six minutes in most areas. The candidates cannot run, as that would be unsafe, and someone will be by their side the whole time in case they have any questions.

Many candidates have to take the tests more than once, and that's okay. Many experienced firefighters say that they learned something new each time they took the test and that each failure just made them more determined to try harder the next time.

The oral interview, while it only lasts for a few minutes, is also an important part of becoming a firefighter and deserves some preparation. During this interview, three officers of the fire department that the candidate is applying to ask them a series of questions that are meant to determine what kind of person the candidate is.

Each candidate needs to spend some time practicing answering the questions honestly and clearly, as well as being clear as to what they will be expected to know. For example, candidates may be asked why they want to be a firefighter, what they expect the job to be like, how they would handle different kinds of problems with fellow firefighters or citizens, and where they see themselves in five years.

Together, these three phases of training (the education, the written exam and physical test, and the oral interview with the officers) all prepare candidates for a life of firefighting and emergency rescue work. Do you think that the training is easy? Not at all. According to one source, about 70% of all people who start training to become firefighters don't finish the process. It is not just a matter of being smart or physically fit- it is also a matter of desire. Being a firefighter (as we will see in the next section) is a challenging job. Each person who decides to make it their career needs to be dedicated to the job and be determined not to give up on both good days and bad days. Becoming a firefighter should be a way of life, and the training process makes sure that everyone understands that.

After over a year of getting ready to become a firefighter and after passing several tests, candidates will apply for a job at their local firehouse. What kind of life can they expect once they have become a firefighter? Let's find out.

Chapter 3: Is Being a Firefighter an Easy Job?

So far, we have learned quite a lot about what firefighters do and about how much training they have to go through before they can start their new career. However, once they have been approved to work as a firefighter and have been assigned to a firehouse, does that mean that they can sit back and take it easy? Are their lives made up of rescuing cats stuck in trees and just riding their shiny trucks in parades? Let's look at some of the working conditions for an average firefighter and you can decide for yourself whether or not it is an easy job.

Aside from the work itself, one of the things that set being a firefighter apart from other jobs is the schedule. For many employees, like teachers, bankers, doctors, and even the bosses of big companies, the work day is made up of a eight or nine hour shift. There is a set time to go in work and a set time to go home. Each night, the employees can be with their families and sleep in their own beds. However, firefighters live according to a different type of schedule.

As you know, emergencies can happen anytime, day or night. Firefighters know this and have decided to organize themselves into different shifts so that there is always a crew of emergency workers at the firehouse ready to help in any emergency. However, firefighters have adopted a schedule where they must stay at the firehouse, ready to go out on an emergency call, for shifts of 24 or 48 hours (one or two whole days). Then, they will take either two or three days off in a row before their next turn comes up. This schedule lets each firefighter be totally focused on his job during those hours and minimizes the chance of an emergency catching anyone unprepared.

Can you imagine staying in a stationhouse for 24 or 48 hours in a row?[4]

However, as you can probably imagine, this schedule can be pretty difficult for some firefighters. Spending so much time away from their families can be tough, especially for those who are married or who have kids. They miss reading stories to their kids at night, eating dinner at home, and sleeping in their own beds. Although most firehouses have beds, kitchens,

---

[4] Image source: http://alexandriava.gov/uploadedImages/fire/info/Sta6.jpg

bathrooms, and gyms for the firefighters to use, it's just not the same as being in their own homes.

Another difficult part of being a firefighter is the constant physical activity. Firefighters must carry heavy equipment and hoses into buildings and carry victims out of them. They must cut holes in cars to release passengers trapped inside and must learn how to push and pull apart ceilings to make sure that there are no hidden fires burning in attics. Not everyone can keep up such a high level of physical activity day in and day out. Firefighters, even when they aren't in the streets helping out during an emergency, must always keep themselves in excellent shape and avoiding doing anything that could make them weaker. Even during their off hours, firefighters try to be safe and protect their health so that they can continue working at the job that they love.

Another difficult part of being a firefighter has to do with the work itself. As we saw in the first section, in one day a firefighter might be expected to handle many different types of emergencies. They might go out to the scene of a car accident to help a victim there, and then an hour later they might have to rescue a child who fell down into a well. Then, later that day, they might put out a house fire and then later visit a school to teach everyone there about fire safety. Not everyone can deal with so many different types of activities at one job, but that is simply part of being a firefighter.

There can be no doubt- being a firefighter has some unique challenges. However, most firefighters will agree that there are also some unique benefits to the job. While firefighters must spend long hours away from their families, they learn to make friends with their crew and form a kind of second family. And just like any other family, these men and women eat together, work together, do chores together, and even sleep under the same roof! And they learn to enjoy having time off when everyone else in the town is at work.

Firefighters also have a real sense of purpose and appreciation for the work that they do. It's true that they have to put forth a lot of effort to stay in shape, but they love helping out their neighbors in the community when they most need it. They love being the people who can arrive in the middle of a tough situation and help to keep everyone calm. Many also love to see the looks on the faces of everyone when they pull up in their truck because everyone knows that it's going to be okay once the firefighters have arrived.

There are some difficult parts of being a firefighter, but for many people around the world, the benefits outweigh the challenges.

Chapter 4: What Is An Average Day Like For a Firefighter?

Firefighters spend their time at work making sure that they are always prepared for any emergency calls that may come in. But they don't just sit there waiting for something to happen. In between emergency calls, firefighters use their time to take care of their equipment and the stationhouse itself. Have you ever wondered what it would be like to spend a whole day as a firefighter? Let's go through an average day at work for a firefighter and see what it's like. Although there are certainly plenty of exciting moments of adventure, you may be surprised to learn that firefighters have chores to do, just like you.

Many firefighters around the country begin their shifts at 8 AM. Those who will be starting a new shift usually arrive a little early (at about 7:30 AM) to speak with the crew from the previous shift and to make sure that, at the stroke of 8, they are already where they are supposed to be.

After talking with the previous crew and finding out where they will be assigned that day during any emergency calls (as a driver, hose man, etc.) the firefighters will do a detailed inspection of the truck and emergency equipment before having a brief meeting with the entire crew to talk about the activities planned for the day. During this meeting, they find out who will go out to inspect buildings, who will visit schools, who will take care of which chores around the stationhouse, and so on.

Some firefighters visit schools to teach kids about fire safety[5]

The first priority of each shift is usually cleaning up the sleeping and eating areas of the stationhouse as well as its restroom. Is it hard for you to imagine highly-trained firefighters scrubbing toilets, making beds, and sweeping the floor? Those chores might not sound fun, but they are important and firefighters are happy to take care of them.

---

[5] Image source: http://www.dailybulldog.com/db/wp-content/uploads/2011/10/firefighter_shakes.jpg

Each firefighter then goes their own way to work on the different tasks that they have been assigned. Some may be sent outside to mow the lawn and to trim the trees and bushes of the stationhouse. One or two other members of the crew may take a special vehicle and go out into the community to visit schools or businesses and educate them about fire safety. Others may be assigned to clean the outside of the stationhouse, to maintain the plumbing and electrical systems, or to do some of the necessary paperwork that keeps everything running smoothly.

However, the very moment that a call comes in, everybody on the crew drops what they are doing, puts on their emergency equipment, goes to the fire truck, and rushes to the scene of the emergency. Even those who are visiting schools or businesses will stop their presentations or inspections and go help. After all, a firefighter is needed most when there are lives at stake. Emergency calls are received through a dispatcher, and the captain will let the dispatcher know whether the fire truck is ready to respond to an emergency or if they are busy helping someone else. Good communication makes sure that help always arrives quickly.

After eating lunch and taking a short break (maybe to call their families or to have a quick nap) the crew will continue in their activities for the afternoon, which might involve receiving additional training for different parts of their job or taking care of other important work around the stationhouse. Most firefighting crews receive at least four emergency calls per day, and sometimes they receive even more. After getting back to the stationhouse after each call, the crew has to make sure that the fire truck is cleaned and that any supplies that were used are restocked so that the truck is ready to go on the next emergency call. If they have to use their hoses to fight a fire, then the hoses must be cleaned, dried, and repacked once the firefighters return to the station.

Firefighters work hard and do not believe in procrastination. Do you know what procrastination is? Procrastination is waiting until later to do something that should be done right now. Firefighters always want to be ready to help out their neighbors, so that means that leaving important preparations until later, like cleaning and maintenance, is not an option. Even though cleaning and maintenance is hard work and sometimes needs to be done in the middle of the night, firefighters always make sure that the hoses are cleaned, the truck is stocked, and the equipment is ready to be used after getting back from each and every emergency. Can you imagine what would happen if a firefighter was woken up in the middle of the night by an alarm but couldn't find his equipment, or how terrible it would be if there were no hoses available for them to put out the fire?

Firefighters try to get some rest at night, but they know that, at any minute, they may be woken up by an alarm. Firefighters spend 24 or 48 hours at the stationhouse during their shifts, and a lot of that time is spent making sure that the people and the equipment (including the trucks) are ready to go at a moment's notice. At the end of their shifts, the firefighters will enjoy two or three days of rest at home with their families, tired but happy to have been able to help.

Chapter 5: What Is the Hardest Part of Being a Firefighter?

Firefighters are seen as heroes by most people, but that doesn't mean that their job is easy. Firefighters have two difficult things to deal with that most other people never have to think about: long hours and dealing with tragedy.

As we saw before, firefighters have to work long hours, often 24 or 48 hour shifts. During that time, they must stay at the stationhouse unless they are working in some other area or helping out during an emergency. Have you ever had to stay away one home for that long of a time? It can be easy to feel a little lonely and homesick during their shifts, but firefighters know how important their jobs are and are willing to make the sacrifice of spending so much time away from their families. Doesn't that make you appreciate the hard work of firefighters even more?

Firefighters also have to learn how to deal with tragedy. For most of us, we will only have to experience something really terrible, like a car accident, once in our lives- or maybe never. We may never have to watch our house burn down, might never have to be cut out of a car, and might never have to be taken to a hospital in the back of an ambulance. However, firefighters deal with those things every day.

Every day, firefighters have to comfort people who have just lost everything in a house fire and have to treat victims of accidents. Sometimes they have to watch people die and help the survivors deal with the pain. Can you imagine what it would be like to be surrounded by so much emotion, day in and day out? Firefighters have to learn how to see and experience terrible things and still stay focused on doing their job. They have to learn to deal with the darker part of life.

Not everyone has what it takes to see so much tragedy and still go to work each day- but firefighters have learned to see sad things and yet to work even harder to make sure that a bad situation doesn't get any worse. They know that, in those dark moments, what people need most is a hero- someone who will help them and who will tell them that everything is going to be okay. We can be thankful to the men and women who put forth so much effort to help out in their communities as firefighters.

Chapter 6: What Does the Future Hold for Firefighters?

New technology, like this robot, will make firefighters even
more effective in the future[6]

---

[6] Image source:
http://www.redorbit.com/news/technology/1112866565/robotic-
firefighter-creates-3d-map-060613/

After all that we have learned, does choosing the career of a firefighter seem like something that you would like to do? Do you think that you have the dedication necessary for the job, and are you willing to work long hours under difficult conditions? If so, then you might wonder what the world of firefighting will be like when you are ready to become one, maybe in ten years or so. Let's have a look at some of the things that are being developed today for use by firefighters, at some of the new technologies that you yourself might get to use someday.

First off, we want to answer the question: "Will we still need firefighters in ten years?" The answer, of course, is yes. Although a lot of things in life will probably be better In the future, there will still be car accidents, medical emergencies, and uncontrolled fires in houses and businesses. Firefighters will still have to be there to help their communities deal with these emergencies, and people will still need brave heroes to rescue them in their most difficult moments. What are some of the new technologies that firefighters will be using in the coming years to help the people of the future?

In the picture at the beginning of this section, you saw a new type of robot that might soon be helping firefighters to save more lives and to fight fires more safely. Using special equipment, a team of these robots will move into a burning structure and look for victims, find out where the fire is the worst, and determine if there are any gas leaks which may cause a large explosion. In just a few minutes, these robots could give firefighters valuable information that will let them save more lives, including their own. When the firefighters move in a few minutes after the robots, they will know what areas to avoid and how to find the people that most need their help.

Another new technology has to do with making better masks.

New masks being designed for firefighters[7]

This new technology (which is still being developed) will help firefighters once they move into a burning building. The helmet (as you can see in the previous picture) helps firefighters to navigate when surrounded by fire. How does it work? Although it has not yet been approved for use everywhere, the helmet uses a special camera that can measure temperature, and

---

[7] Image source: http://hudsandguis.com/2013/03/20/c-thru-smoke-helmet/

then, in a special display, it shows the firefighter where the hottest parts of the fire are. It even shows them where the walls of a building are located so that the rescue workers can walk around safely. Instead of carrying heavy measuring equipment with them that might slow them down, rescue workers will have their hands free and will be able to move more quickly to find victims and pull them to safety. This new mask is also important because, inside most burning buildings, the smoke is so thick that firefighters have trouble seeing and sometimes lose valuable time finding the victim and the fire. The new technology on this mask will help them to move more quickly and get the job done faster and more safely.

Another important tool being used by fire crews across the country has to do with research and investigation. These crews are working on understanding how fires today are different than fires that burned twenty years ago. As you may already know, fires burn faster or slower depending on what's around it. If there are large spaces and materials made of plastic, then the fires will burn hotter and faster. Homes today are built using different materials, designs, and are filled with different furniture than houses built in the past. Today, fire crews find abandoned houses and set fire to them to see how the fire acts and spreads. They test their equipment inside and make sure that the firefighters can survive the heat. Then, they use the information that they have learned to make sure that they are prepared for every type of fire. These methods make sure that fire crews are always up to date with their methods. In the future, building methods and designs will continue to change, so experiments like this will be valuable in saving lives and houses.

Another tool that might be used more in the future helps fire captains to keep track of where their crew is when inside a burning building. Like a GPS unit, the tool shows little dots as they move through a building, so that a captain can give clear directions to his crew during the emergency.

The display shows where the firefighters are inside of a building[8]

This tool can be helpful is a firefighter is injured or if there is so much noise that the firefighters can't hear each other yelling. By knowing the

---

[8] Image source: http://www.trxsystems.com/GPS-Denied-Navigation-Products/

exact location of everyone at each moment, the fire crews will work together better as a team and can help each other out more quickly.

Finally, have a look at the following picture of a technology that firefighters may soon be using when handling emergencies.

A pair of special robotic legs makes it easier to carry heavy equipment[9]

---

[9] Image source: http://bleex.me.berkeley.edu/research/exoskeleton/bleex/

Can you tell what is happening in that picture? In California, the University of Berkeley has developed something exciting that may help firefighters to climb lots of stairs with heavy equipment without getting tired- an exoskeleton. Two robotic legs attach to the firefighter's real legs and can help them to climb lots of stairs, to carry heavy hoses and oxygen tanks, and to drag out victims without getting as tired. This

exciting new tool might be used in the future to help firefighters do more than they ever could before, with just one person doing the work of three or four. Can you imagine how amazing that would be to see?

Firefighting will be just as important in ten years as it is today, but we can expect that new technology will make firefighters more effective than ever and will help them to save even more lives. However, as we have seen, the thing that makes a good firefighter is not really the equipment that they use- although that is important. What makes a good firefighter is the kind of person that they are. A good firefighter is a person who is ready to work hard and to give of themselves for others. They are willing to rush into a dangerous area when everyone else is trying to get away. So no matter what kind of new technology is used to fight fires and save lives, one thing will always remain the same-firefighters will need to be brave and courageous heroes.

Chapter 7: How Can You Get Ready Now to Become a Firefighter?

There is no doubt that being a firefighter is a hugely exciting and rewarding career for those who choose it. Those who spend their lives helping others deserve all of our thanks and respect. After considering the first six sections, do you find yourself thinking seriously about becoming a firefighter too? If so, then you probably want to know what you can do now to get ready. As we saw earlier, you must be at least eighteen and have finished your basic education before taking the tests and going to the academy. But there are several ways that you can prepare yourself now for a life of heroism.

1) A great first step is to try and adopt the right attitude. Firefighters have good pay and great benefits, but most people who sign up to become firefighters do so because they truly want to help others. So why not start learning how to help others right now by volunteering in your community? Ask your guidance counselor or a trusted adult for ideas of how you can spend your time after school helping others. They may suggest lots of ideas, and you can start by choosing one and seeing how you like it. For example, you might tutor younger students, spend time with older people at a retirement home, or work at a local chapter of the Red Cross teaching CPR. If there is a nearby camp for kids who are burn victims, why not see if you can volunteer your time playing games with and helping the kids who go there? And if your community has a homeless shelter, see what

kind of help they need. You might be asked to cook, to clean, or to organize donated clothing. No matter what you end up doing, you will be helping out your neighbors.

Although you won't make any money volunteering, you will be rewarded as you start to see how good it feels to give back to the community and to be a part of something bigger than yourself. While other kids surf the internet, send text messages, or play video games, you can spend a couple of hours per week making a real difference in someone's life, just like firefighters do every day that they goes to work.

2) Do your best to develop a good work ethic at home and be sure to stay out of trouble with the police. Doing drugs or getting arrested are quick ways to miss out on ever becoming a firefighter. On the other hand, having a solid reputation will make it easier for you to get accepted into the academy and to get a job as a firefighter later

on. Behave yourself at home as well and learn the importance of doing chores (like cooking, cleaning, and washing dishes), as this will help you to be a productive member of any fire crew that you are assigned to. And try your best to avoid procrastinating, even if what you have to do doesn't seem like much fun.

3) Experienced firefighters also recommend starting to learn as much as you can right now about the rescue operations and day-to-day life of a firefighter. Do you personally know any firefighters? Can you visit a local stationhouse to meet some and ask them about their job? Also, try to understand the whole process that your local stationhouse uses to hire new firefighters. Although we covered the main details here, sometimes local crews have a certain order or some specific suggestions that they want everyone to follow. So take some time to investigate. Also, ask if they have a program that will let you be a volunteer firefighter. That way,

you can learn lots of valuable information and see if firefighting actually is the career for you.

4) Earlier, we saw how firefighters are expected to be in terrific physical shape in order to be effective at their jobs. They must take a test before they can get hired and they must stay in terrific shape to be able to carry hoses and victims around. Instead of waiting until you are older to get in fantastic shape, why not talk to your doctor now and listen to his or her advice on how you can get in better shape. Your doctor will recommend the best foods to eat, safe exercises you can do, and even how much sleep you should get each night. When exercising, remember that your focus should be on developing the strength to do the job of a firefighter. This means lots of heavy lifting and endurance- and not so much running and speed. You can get some suggestions on how to get ready for the firefighter Physical Ability Test

(PAT) at the following website:

http://lincoln.ne.gov/city/fire/employ/pat.pdf.

Although you may still have quite a few years left until you can officially apply to become a firefighter, don't let any more time go by without at least starting to get ready, if this is indeed the career that you want. Train your mind and body now, and later you will be able to use them to help out your community as a heroic firefighter!

Conclusion

Wow! We learned a lot about firefighters in this book. They are incredibly brave men and women who spend their lives giving to others and putting themselves in danger to save their neighbors. Can you think of a better job than that? What impressed you most about the life of a firefighter? What was your favorite part of this book? Let's have a quick review of all of the fascinating things that we learned.

First, we found out more about what firefighters do. While a lot of people think that firefighters only rush into burning buildings, we saw that their jobs include many more activities than that. Firefighters are expected to have good reputations and to serve the communities that they live in. They help out in all kinds of emergency situations and even try to prevent emergencies by educating people at schools and businesses in the area that they serve.

Then we learned about the specialized training that each person has to go through before they can become a firefighter. We saw the intensive training that involves both the mind and the body, and how a high level of physical performance and a lot of knowledge is expected from each potential firefighter. Only about 30% of the people who start training to become firefighters end up finishing the training, which lasts over one year. Along with a complete education that teaches the students about first aid, the behavior of fire, and building structures, the students must pass a physical exam, an oral exam, and a written exam.

The third section showed us more of the reality of being a firefighter by answering the question:

is being a firefighter an easy job? We looked at several aspects of this unique job and tried to decide whether or not just anyone can come in off the street and start working as a firefighter. You would probably agree with anyone who says that it is not an easy job. From the specialized shifts to the intense physical requirements, there are some specific challenges that firefighters have to deal with, and it is not a job for just anyone.

Then we got an exciting look at the average day of a firefighter. We got to see what it's like to stay at the stationhouse, ride along on emergency calls, and participate in the many different areas of being a firefighter. While you may have had an idea of what a firefighter does with their time all day, weren't you surprised to find out that being a firefighter is more than just running into burning buildings? A lot of people are shocked when they find out that a good firefighter has to be able both to save lives and to scrub toilets!

The fifth section talked honestly about the hardest part of being a firefighter. Although firefighters are expected to keep the stationhouse clean, to work long hours, and to be in great physical shape, the hardest part for most firefighters is something completely unrelated: dealing with the tragedies of life that they come across in their jobs. Firefighters have to see some terrible things sometimes, and it's not always easy to control the emotions that come up. But isn't it true that we appreciate the men and women who are willing to be with us during the ugly times and during the accidents? Imagine how sad the world would be if nobody came to help us when we needed them most.

Then we looked down the road into the future to try and see what the career of a firefighter will be like in ten years, right about the time that you might consider it for yourself. We answered the question of whether or not firefighters will still be needed in ten years and then we looked at some recent inventions that might be used to make firefighters even better at their jobs. We saw a new face mask that will let the rescue workers see through the smoke and find victims; we saw a robot that clears a path for firefighters; we saw a special way of tracking the movement of crews inside a structure; and we saw a new exoskeleton that will allow firefighters to climb stairs and walk long distances while carrying heavy equipment, all without tiring out as much. Being a firefighter in the future will be even more exciting than it is today.

Finally, the seventh and final section answered the important question "How can you get ready now to become a firefighter". Even though firefighters must be eighteen years old in most states, there are several things that you can do right now to get ready. We talked about how you can prepare yourself physically and mentally right now, so that when you are eighteen you can start the process to becoming a firefighter. Have you decided what you will do first? Will you start volunteering, visiting stationhouses, or educating yourself further about the life of a firefighter? Whatever you choose, don't let any more time go by without doing something!

The world needs heroes- people who are willing to step in and do what's needed. Do you have what it takes to be a hero? If so, then maybe becoming a firefighter is the career for you. Learn how to give of yourself to others and how to be a team player. In no time, you will experience the thrill that comes with helping others in their time of need, just like a firefighter!

76715870R00038

Made in the USA
Columbia, SC
10 September 2017